Leadership in a Box: Developing a Networking Organization

Leadership in a Box: Developing a Networking Organization

William H. Bishop, DSL

Leadership in a Box: Developing a Networking Organization by William H. Bishop
© 2016 William H. Bishop. ALL RIGHTS RESERVED. No part of this book may be reproduced in any form or by any means, electronic, mechanical, digital, photocopying, or recording, except for inclusion of a review, without permission in writing from the publisher or Author. Some images were purchased from Adobe Stock Royalty Free Images.

Published in the USA by:
Bishop Advisory Group
Virginia Beach, VA
ISBN-13: 978-1523373581
ISBN-10: 152337358X
Printed in the United States of America

This book is dedicated to the professors, faculty, and staff of Regent University, who mentored and guided me on my doctoral journey!

Also by William H. Bishop:

Going Home: A Networking Survival Guide

The Currency of Leadership

Table of Contents

Foreword 9

Introduction 13

Organizational Structure, Systems, and Environment 15

Strategic Planning, Design, and Implementation 21

The Human Focus of Leadership 27

Leadership Theory and Development 33

Global Strategic Leadership 39

Innovation and Creativity 45

Values and Ethics 51

The Future of Organizational Design 57

Who's Next? 63

Servant Networking: Opening the Box 67

Foreword

Large corporations in the United States are discovering that their cumbersome organizations are ill-equipped to compete in the dynamic global marketplace. Based on historical organizational designs of the military, railroads, and mills, their moribund hierarchical structures consistently impede rapid communications, efficient resource allocation, and crucial innovation. These lumbering dinosaurs are losing the productivity race to the hare *and* the tortoise.

William Bishop has written *Leadership in a Box: Developing a Networking Organization* as a near-manifesto of what is needed to get corporations back into the global battle royal. Dr. Bishop strongly recognizes the importance of individual people to the success of companies and views the leader's primary role as connecting employees to each other and helping them achieve their best work. The fundamental goal of leadership is to help the organization willingly succeed *en toto* by promoting relationships and connections.

Simply flattening the organizational structure is not new, nor sufficient. Dr. Bishop recounts how companies like W. L. Gore, Zappos, and Valve Corporation used teamwork and peer accountability as they viewed their companies as far more than the sum of its parts. As the Japanese are wont to say, "None of us is as smart as all of us."

What makes the work of Dr. Bishop so intriguing are two key ideas. First is that the relentless march of technology and the burgeoning Internet have already begun to encourage the natural development of both formal and informal information channels and relationships throughout the organization, subsidiaries, suppliers, and customers. Instant messaging, Twitter, smartphones, and social networking sites are all useful in this new connectivity. Do you have a question about the durability of a product? Pick up your handheld and immediately connect to an associate in Bangalore or Munich for the appropriate information. By building and promoting deep partnerships, the information is mutually beneficial for personal and corporate success.

Second, and of most importance to what Bill Bishop has labeled "servant networking," is the unique and important role of leaders to organizational success. Extending the notable work on servant leadership by

Robert Greenleaf, Bishop demonstrates that the desire of leaders to serve others can be accomplished by harnessing the formidable power of networking to link people together for the greater good. Successful leaders *serve* their networks so that all may survive and succeed. *Leadership in a Box* ably echoes one of the first works of Poet Laureate Robert Frost entitled *The Tuft of Flowers*:
'Men work together,' I told him from the heart,
'Whether they work together or apart.'

Dr. Gary Oster
Regent University
School of Business & Leadership
Virginia Beach, VA
September 2016

Introduction

Servant networking involves serving others and helping them achieve all they are capable of achieving. Servant networkers are leaders who think in terms of what they can do for other people, specifically connecting them to other people. The more they give to those in their network, the more they will receive in return and the stronger and more mutually beneficial it will become for those in it (Bishop, 2013, p. 102-103).

Leadership is fundamentally about people. It encompasses their attitudes, behaviors, and interactions with others, and directly contributes to job satisfaction and quality of life. Organizations are comprised of people. Global organizations are represented in different countries and cultures. A myriad of cultures, norms, and beliefs are reflected within individual organizational units of a single nation. Globalization has all but erased national borders, and it has blurred cultural boundaries. Leaders have been challenged to rise to the occasion, adopt new strategies, and implement change in order to meet the demands of the global economy and remain relevant. Technological advancements have transformed the organizational landscape. Global communication resides within the palm of one's hand via smartphone technology. Information now flows around the world in milliseconds. Leaders have struggled to keep pace. The hierarchies that reigned supreme yesterday have been flattened in an attempt to streamline the flow of information, simplify processes, and make organizations global contenders. A new form of leadership integration and organizational structure is required for the organization of the future. This paper will discuss the implementation of servant networking as a leadership method, organizational structure, and strategy for developing a networking organization. It will provide examples of how servant leadership, influence, and integrated networks affect the daily operations and long-term success of an organization. An understanding of these concepts within the global construct is vital to organizational survival. Additionally, this paper posits the idea that the aforementioned leadership concepts can be organized in a systematic approach and packaged for successful implementation within an organization—in a box, as it were.

Organizational Structure, Systems, and Environment

Organizations are comprised of an internal structure that allows them to manage the flow of communication and compartmentalize information in a systematic manner in the name of efficiency. The composition of the structure both vertically and horizontally establishes the overall design. In modern organizations, "design shapes the patterns of information processing" (Nadler & Tushman, 1997, p. 64). Intricate structures contain many levels through which information must be disseminated. This can delay the request approval process, lead to incorrect decisions being made due to a lack of information, cause disheartened employees, and create misalignment (Ashkenas, Ulrich, Jick, & Kerr, 2002).

In addition to providing a systematic method of communication and information management, structure identifies the distribution of power within the organization in two ways. "The first is the vertical distribution of decision-making power and authority" (Galbraith, 2002, p. 22). This determines the centralization, or decentralization, within the structure and establishes a pecking order. "The second is the horizontal distribution of power [in which] the leader needs to shift power to the department dealing with mission-critical issues" (Galbraith, 2002, p. 22).

As far as organizational structures go, the hierarchy has firmly established its place in organizational history:

> Hierarchies are, as they have been for centuries, 'normal' and prevalent everywhere. The hierarchical pyramid is probably the single element we are most likely to envision when we hear the word *organization*. Hierarchies pervade democracies, theocracies, oligarchies, monarchies, and autocracies (Leavitt, 2004, p. 1-2).

While hierarchies have their place in organizational history, they are not without their pitfalls. The "levels in a hierarchy potentially lead to distortions in the transmission of information and implementation delays, while spans of control are limited by how much information a manager can process" (Guadalupe & Wulf, 2010, p. 106).

In order to combat some of these negative consequences, some organizations have adopted a flat structure. "Firms are flattening their corporate hierarchies. Spans of control have broadened and the number of levels within firms has declined" (Guadalupe et al, 2010, p. 106). Although firms have flattened their hierarchies, they have not abandoned their structure. "Flatness of organizational structure describes an organization's relative number of management levels in the chain of command" (Huang, Mehmet, M. K., & Roger, 2010, p. 517). Levels still exist. However, their number is significantly reduced in order to promote expediency and eliminate the stagnation of information.

Organizations are changing their structures and creating interconnected circles of influence, known as Holacracy, which are replacing hierarchical levels. Valve Corporation, a video-game maker in Bellevue, WA, is one example of a company where hierarchies do not exist:

> At Valve, there are no promotions, only new projects. To help decide pay, employees rank their peers—but not themselves—voting on who they think creates the most value. Any employee can participate in hiring decisions,

which are usually made by teams. Firings, while relatively rare, work the same way: teams decide together if someone isn't working out (Silverman, 2012).

Morning Star, a leading food processor, is a company where the internal structure is dependent on peer-group accountability. In regard to the organization's structure, founder Chris Rufer (as cited in Hamel, 2011, p. 53) stated, "Around here, nobody's your boss and everybody's your boss." Another example of a company where traditional structure has been replaced is Gore. "W.L. Gore and Associates Inc., the maker of Gore-Tex fabric, is organized as a loose network of employees responsible to each other and their projects but lacking job titles. Bill Gore, the company founder, dubs this a 'lattice' structure" (Jeffrey & Brian, 2008, p. 82). Peer-group accountability and the use of teams is a common theme among such organizations. These themes correspond to the integration of networking as an organizational structural component.

Networks as structural components provide decisive advantages over traditional structures. "No traditional corporate structure, regardless of how decluttered [sic] or delayered [sic], can muster the speed, flexibility, and focus that success today demands. Networks are faster, smarter, and more flexible" (Charan, 1991, p. 104-105). Their use is not limited to the confines of a single organization. Inter-organizational networking is being utilized in order to create alliances. "Strategic interorganizational alliances and networking (through technology) are becoming the keys in managing organizations in the 1990s. Many firms (both small and large) have now realized the need for business alliances" (Zeffane, 1994p. 28). Indeed, alliances and relationships are becoming a strategic component for survival in the global economy.

Strategic Planning, Design, and Implementation

Organizational strategy sets the tone and direction for an organization and creates value (de Kluyver & Pearce II, 2009). It is the battle plan by which corporations wage war on the global landscape. An organization's strategy must compliment its structure because "structure follows strategy" (Mintzberg, Ahlsrand, & Lample, 1998, p. 35). The two must be interwoven so as to be indistinguishable from each other. Strategy is built upon strategic thinking, which is "the cognitive processes required for the collection, interpretation, generation, and evaluation of information and ideas that shape an organization's sustainable competitive advantage" (Hughes & Beatty, 2005, p. 44). It is "a distinctive management activity whose purpose is to discover novel, imaginative strategies which can rewrite the rules of the competitive game; and to envision potential futures significantly different from the present" (Goldman, 2007, p. 75-76). Strategic thinking is not reserved for senior leadership. It is incumbent that everyone in an organization be involved in the process because strategic thinking involves systems thinking, creativity, and vision. Kaufman (as cited in Bonn, 2005, p. 338) noted that systems thinking was "a switch from seeing the organization as a splintered conglomerate of disassociated parts (and employees) competing for resources, to seeing and dealing with the corporation as a holistic system that integrates each part in relationship to the whole." In other words, an organization is comprised of substructures, each of which must function as a separate entity within the confines of the whole.

These sub-structures are a critical component in the overall structure of an organization because they generate creativity, which is a vital element in the strategic development of an organization. "Strategy is about ideas and the development of novel solutions to create competitive advantage. Strategic thinkers must search for new approaches and envision better ways of doing things, in other words, be creative" (Bonn, 2005, p. 338). Organizational leaders need to think outside the proverbial box and tap into the creative pool of talent within the organization by encouraging strategic thinking because it "results in creative ways for a company to develop" (Belardo, Duchessi, & Coleman, 1994, p. 135). This is critical for the next step in the process, strategic planning. "Mintzberg argues that strategic planning and thinking involve two distinct thought processes: planning concerns analysis establishing and formalizing systems and procedures; thinking involves synthesis—encouraging intuitive, innovative and creative thinking at all levels of the organization" (Graetz, 2002, p. 456).

The combination of strategic thinking and strategic planning form an organization's overall strategy. While strategic thinking is predicated upon the cognitive process of developing creative solutions, strategic planning is "the ability to focus the attention of all organizational members on a common set of significant long-term issues" (Liedtka, 1998, p. 34). Planning provides the direction and application of the thinking process. This is significant for the development and implementation of a networking organization, which relies upon the interconnectivity of people in order to fulfill the vision and mission. Networking must be an inherent component of the strategic thinking and planning of the organization in order to establish a corresponding structural base.

The use of networking as part of an organization's strategic thinking and planning has gained momentum in the past two decades. Zeffane (1995) observed, "Strategic alliances and networks have become an integral part of contemporary strategic organizational thinking" (p. 26). Networks promote collaboration and the sharing of information, and they empower the right people to make timely, key decisions. Charan (1991) observed:

> A network reshapes how and by whom essential business decisions get made. It integrates decisions horizontally at the lowest managerial levels and with superior speed. In effect, a network identifies the "small company inside the large company" and empowers it to make the four-dimensional trade-offs—among functions, business units, geography, and global customers—that determine success in the marketplace. It enables the right people in the organization to converge faster and in a more focused way than the competition on operating priorities determined by the imperatives of meeting customer needs and building concrete advantage (p. 105).

Networking is a fundamental component of human interaction. Relationships are at the heart of networking.

They comprise the foundations upon which networks are built. As such, they should be integrated into the strategic thinking and planning of organizations. Networking is becoming a predominant work pattern among organizations (Wills, 1994). Human interaction is the sine qua non of organizational strategy. Leaders must harness the power of relationships in order to maximize their strategic effectiveness.

The Human Focus of Leadership

After strategic thinking has been completed and a plan has been developed, it must be implemented. This is accomplished by organizational personnel. From the CEO down, implementing the strategic plan ultimately falls on people. The human element is an organizational imperative from which no organization can escape. Therefore, it is incumbent upon leaders to harness the power of human interaction via networks to get the job done. "In any group, formal structure and informal networks coexist, each influencing how people get their jobs done" (Battilana & Casciaro, 2013, p. 64). Within the confines of every organization, informal networks exist. Some may refer to them as the grapevine, rumor mill, or scuttlebutt. The term used is irrelevant. What is relevant is the impact such networks can have.

Though the people in these networks often have little or no formally identified power, they wield tremendous influence within the organization. In regard to those in the informal networks, Cialdini (2013) noted, "We're not talking about being *in* authority but about *an* authority" (p. 78). Influence can quickly make one an authority because it "is one of the most powerful skills around. It allows us instantly to earn the trust and respect of others, and lead and manage teams, individuals and situations with power, confidence and success" (Clayton, 2011, p. x). Influence is one of the elements that makes networking such a powerful force within an organization.

Harnessing the power of these *influencers* is critical for sustained leadership within an organization. "Effective influencers understand that what shapes and sustains the behavioral norms of an organization are lots of small interactions" (Grenny, Maxfield, & Shimberg, 2008, p. 51). These are the people who—having no formal authority, title, or position—walk the halls on a daily basis. They visit cubicles, hang out in the break room, and engage in brief conversations with many employees. In other words, they network! They build relationships and harness their power.

They serve as both mentors and consultants to others within the organization. Block (1981) stated, "A consultant is a person in a position to have some influence over an individual, a group, or an organization, but who has no direct power to make changes or implement programs" (p. 2). This is precisely what is occurring in organizations today. The *influencers* are spreading information, generating the formation of opinions, and impacting the success of organizations through the development and use of networks. It is critical that organizational leaders fully understand and utilize these networks because "peers are often more convincing than executives" (Cialdini, 2013, p. 79). What better way to transmit information, mission, and vision than through an informal network!

In addition to the timely dissemination of information, networks empower those in them. Empowerment is "moving decision making down to the lowest level where competent decisions can be made" (Fullam, Lando, Johansen, Reyes, & Szaloczy, 1998, p. 254). It is created through the informal proliferation of information and the opportunity to candidly render opinions within the confines of a peer group. Promoting such empowerment is an indispensible facet of strong leaders, and it builds solid networks. As Miller (1995) noted, "The strongest people we really want to involve in our networks are the people who can say 'no' to us" (p. 52). Inviting people to speak openly and honestly provides accurate feedback.

In addition to serving as empowered consultants within an organization, influencers act as informal mentors within their networks. Informal mentorship occurs in an environment of trust. "Trust is a crucial commodity throughout a mentor relationship" (Bell, 2002, p. 41). Within any organization, circles of trust exist among peer groups and adjacent levels of the structure. It is in these circles that information is often exchanged with influence added. People are driven to achieve. As a result, they have "a need to measure up, to do well, to succeed. Many people are driven by a need for affirmation, and the adoration of others" (Bell, 2002, p. 51). They find acceptance, recognition, and affirmation in their informal networks as they consult with and mentor one another. They directly influence the daily tone of the organization.

Technology has increased the communication ability of people in these informal networks, which has exponentially expanded their influence. The proliferation of social media has had a direct impact on the influence of informal networks. Even in the workplace, employees are connected socially and can instantly express concern or indignation via social media. Serena, a California software company, has "implemented 'Facebook Fridays' which allows employees a free hour every Friday to update their Facebook profiles and keep in touch online with colleagues" (Bennett, Owers, Pitt, & Tucker, 2010, p. 145). Social networking has given everyone a voice. Additionally, it has streamlined the flow of information. "With the advent of smart-phones, during times of a company or civil emergency, a manager no longer needs to call a multitude of individuals, they only need to send a tweet using Twitter.com or other [social networking service] and can instantly connect with their particular following" (Johnson, 2011, p. 8). This same instant connectivity can be used to spread organizational information, i.e. the hiring of a new person, and opinion, i.e. the expression of dissatisfaction with a supervisor. Johnson (2011) aptly concluded:

> The industrial revolution shrunk the world, the electronic age has compressed time, and Social Networking has greatly enlarged the audience and shifted the power structure in favor of the customer or individual. Leaders need to master the technology and concepts of Web 2.0 now. (p. 8-9).

Indeed, leaders must integrate social networking technology with leadership theory in order to leverage the power of technology and informal organizational networks.

Leadership Theory and Development

The world of academia is replete with leadership theories and concepts. Leadership is often an all-encompassing idea meant to capture beliefs, ideals, and expectations of those charged with the development of others. Northouse (2007) defines leadership as "a process" that "involves influence, occurs in a group context, and involves goal attainment. Process implies that a leader affects and is affected by followers" (p. 3). Leadership is incumbent upon followership. After all, no one leads all of the time. Leaders follow other leaders, and are therefore part-time followers. Followership is a fundamental principle of leadership and a key element of networking.

To get a better understanding of the leader/follower relationship, consider the strategy involved in a flock of ducks flying in V formation, making sure to keep an eye on the leader:

> Whichever one is up front is working the hardest, [and] will make a strategic switch. The leader will drop back—usually all the way back, where wind drag is lowest, and a rested duck will come to the front. While there is no single, unchanging leader for a V

> of birds on the move, it is the oldest, experienced individuals who are calling the navigational shots, using the sun and the stars at night to orient themselves and stay on course (Zidbits Media, n.d.).

This perfectly exemplifies how leaders serve as followers and followers serve as leaders. It also illustrates the necessity of followership for leadership success (Kelley, 1992). Furthermore, it lends support to the concept of a networking organization. Networks function as a series of interconnected units within the larger construct of an organization. Individuals in the networks experience multiple connections simultaneously, which allows them to function as leaders and followers concomitantly. Chaleff (2009) stated, "The dual role of follower and leader gives us ample opportunity to learn to perform better in both roles" (p. 33). Indeed it does. It also directly impacts the usefulness and effectiveness of communication within an organization.

Fulfilling such a dual role first requires leadership. The style and type of leadership in an organization is predicated upon its culture. "Culture is a set of values, norms, guiding beliefs, and understandings that is shared by members of an organization and is taught to new members" (Daft, 2007, p. 361). Several things including size and demographic composition determine an organization's culture. It is incumbent upon leadership, though, to develop a culture of inclusion in which the dissemination of information can flow expeditiously through both formal and informal channels.

One particular style of leadership well-suited to this objective is the leader-member exchange (LMX). LMX "is centered on the interactions between leaders and followers" (Northhouse, 2007, p. 151). These interactions lead to the development of 'in-groups' and 'out-groups.' "In-group members are willing to do more than is required in their job description and look for innovative ways to advance the group's goals" (Northouse, 2007, p. 158). In-group members exist and operate within the confines of multiple networks, which extends their influence in the organization by affording them contact with out-group members from other networks. "Out-group members operate strictly within their prescribed organizational roles" (Northouse, 2007, p. 158). So while out-group members may not be part of one network, they can be part of others.

Pursuing this concept further is the leadership-making theory, which stipulates that "leaders should develop high-quality exchanges with all of his or her subordinates rather than just a few" (Northouse, 2007, p. 155). This process occurs over time and in phases, the last of which is the mature partnership phase (Northouse, 2007). During this phase, mutually beneficial high value exchanges occur, which is a benefit to the organization (Camplin, 2009). Leadership-making transcends the limitations of LMX's in-groups and out-groups. It "focuses on the methods of earning incremental influence (influence over and above that contained within a role-specified situation) with another unit (individual or group)" (Graen & Uhl-Bien, 1991, p. 25). This influence is vital in order for networks to develop and flourish within an organization. Leaders must seek to develop mature partnerships within the expanse of organizational networks as part of the leader-making process.

In essence, leaders must become servants. They must learn to simultaneously lead and serve, which are mutually inclusive principles of servant leadership. Spears (1996) noted that servant leadership is a balance between service and leading. In regard to servant leadership, Greenleaf stated, "The servant-leader is servant first... It begins with the natural feeling that one wants to serve, to serve first. Then conscious choice brings one to aspire to lead." (Boone & Makhani, 2012, p. 83). These concepts compliment LMX theory and are easily integrated based on the commonality of relationships. "In LMX theory, high-LMX leaders develop trusting and mutually beneficial relationships with employees, just as servant leaders develop strong supportive relationships with all employees and colleagues" (Barbuto & Wheeler, 2006, p. 303). Relationships are the foundation of networking—in this case, servant networking. They provide the means and opportunity for influence. Utilizing the principles of LMX and servant leadership will increase a leader's overall influence within the organization, which is an essential for the success of global organizations.

Global Strategic Leadership

In the global frontier, organizational boundaries are no longer defined in terms of geographic location. They have become global and now span the world. More than merely having an international presence, global organizations are now fully immersed in the cultures of other countries. The technological revolution has connected nations, cultures, and economies. "Globalization has come about through advancement in computer and communications technology with the consequent expansion of free markets with the following benefits: rising global living standards, economic efficiency, individual freedom and democracy, and unprecedented technological progress" (Ardalan, 2009, p. 518). The world is now connected like no other time in history. Disparate cultures are less foreign than in previous decades. Similarities are emphasized and promoted while differences remain in the distance and elusive. "The effect of globalization has been one of ignoring cultural differences and creating sameness. While it has not, and cannot, remove the barriers of language, it has nullified many cultural differences" (Bishop, 2014, p. 5). Globalization has had a profoundly unifying effect on cultures.

"Culture roots and anchors us; it identifies and locates us in the world" (Rosen, 2000, p. 22). It makes us who we are and brands us. Culture conveys ideals, beliefs, ethics, and values. Individual cultures are represented across a geographic spectrum that disassociates location with intrinsic value. "Culture is no longer associated with a fixed locality, but gains new meanings that reflect dominant themes emerging in a global context. This cultural globalization challenges parochial values and identities, because it undermines the association of culture to a fixed location" (Ardalan, 2009, p. 525). In other words, culture has lost some of its uniqueness within its previously contained localities due to the proliferation of globalization. This presents a challenge for today's global executives, who are tasked with overcoming cultural differences and finding commonality in order to advance their organizational vision. As McCall and Hollenbeck (2002) noted, "These global executives work across borders... All of those border crossings contribute to the complexity of the global job" (p. 22).

Organizations must exist simultaneously within different geographic borders and cultures and at the same time maintain their own individuality and organizational culture. They must blend in with the local culture while maintaining brand identity that is predicated on transparency of organizational culture. At the same time, the organization must create and develop a culture that meets these needs. Developing a networking organization will facilitate cultural integration by promoting global thinking "where people are adept at exchanging ideas, processes, and systems across borders" (Marquardt & Berger, 2000, p. 19). Networking creates interconnected circles of influence that are able to transcend the boundaries of culture. It provides a mechanism for harnessing the power of globalization in which the ubiquitous electronic connectivity can be utilized in order to expedite the flow of information—literally around the world. The Luksic Group, based in Chile, has harnessed the power of networking to improve the flow of information. CEO Guillermo Luksic stated, "Our challenge is to build a network of relationships and information channels through subsidiaries and partnerships. Now that we are international, we continue building and improving our network so it's equally strong throughout the region" (Rosen, 2000, p. 132).

In addition to the technological web globalization has weaved, national economies are now united. Economies have become interdependent:

> This refers to the fact that in the globalization era, events that take place in a given country have an immediate and direct impact on other countries. Countries and societies no longer live and operate as isolated self-sustained entities. In addition, these events influence the business operations and market position of corporations (Ali, 2001, p. 6).

The world is connected via the global economy. Organizations rise and fall based on both national and foreign market transactions. Financial collapses have far-reaching consequences that extend beyond national borders. The connectivity that affords organizations the opportunity to flourish can also be the catalyst of their demise. Yet it is this same connectivity that demands a corresponding system of organizational design.

The infrastructure necessary to foster global networking currently exists within the construct of the global economy. The birth of globalization brought with it the necessity to cross cultural boundaries and connect economies. Organizations must leverage the connectivity integration within the global economic construct in order to promote the free exchange of information, collaboration, the development of alliances, and the acquisition of knowledge (Linehan & Scullion, 2008). "Networking forms an essential dimension of organizational life" (Linehan et al, 2008, p. 34) and can now occur in milliseconds via technology. Text messaging, Twitter, and Facebook provide organizations with the ability to connect with thousands of people with the click of a mouse. Across the country, schools, businesses, and even the military use social media to provide emergency information such as weather-related closings and delays to their personnel (Johnson, 2011). Social media has become a significant networking tool for global organizations. Sinclaire and Vogus (2011) observed:

> Facebook now has 500 million users, proclaiming the 35-and-over age group to be the fastest growing demographic. Neilsen reports that time spent on social network and blogging sites is growing at more than three times the rate of overall Internet

growth (p. 294).

Social media is not only impacting how organizations network and disseminate information; its use and strategic incorporation is an essential element of innovative capacity within the global environment.

Innovation and Creativity

As globalization continues to impact how organizations develop and function, they must adapt in order to remain competitive and viable. They must find new ways to communicate and share information. They must innovate and employ creativity. So which came first, creativity or innovation? That is a matter of perspective and interpretation. However, Lewis and Wright (2012) noted, "Innovation is structured creativity focused on producing an innovative product, service, or system. In essence it is a 'practical creativity.'" (p. 9). A measure of creativity is necessary in order to innovate. "Creativity is a subcomponent of the innovation process, and is focused on divergent ideas. Whereas the purpose of innovation is to use divergent ideas towards a convergent solution that is both highly novel and useful." (Lewis et al, 2012, p. 10). In other words, creativity fuels innovation. It serves as the starting point and provides the fabric into which ideas are sewn.

Innovation is "the ability to create new technique or strategy" (Setyawati, Mohd Noor, & Mohammad, 2011, p. 150). Organizations must create new strategies to improve and expedite the flow of information and the generation of ideas. They must find innovative ways of doing business in the global economy, which is predicated on the use of technology to communicate, share ideas, and conduct transactions. Networking is an innovative method for communicating and circumventing the limitations of traditional organizational structures such as the hierarchy. Combined with social media, networking provides a venue for employees to voice opinions, share information, and communicate informally at will. Meetings are not required for the sharing of information. Technology has sidestepped the traditional medium of formal gatherings for the collective sharing of ideas. Creativity flows through cyberspace via social networking. "Basic social networking mechanisms equip users with the ability to form online contacts, join special interest groups, upload and share documents" (Sawant & Wang, 2011,p. 218). Information travels at the speed of light. Ideas are born in the blink of an eye and can die just as quickly.

  Creativity can happen anywhere at anytime. Thoughts can be transmitted and shared with the click of a mouse or the touch of a screen. New policies can be generated from remote locations. Marketing concepts can be developed in the far corners of the world. The incorporation of social media into networking provides instant communication within one's circles of influence. Creativity is a social process (Ohly, Kase, & Skerlavaj, 2010). It gains traction and momentum through the sharing of ideas with others, who in turn expound upon those ideas and use them as the impetus for their own creativity. "By communicating with others, individuals get access to novel perspectives and unique knowledge" (Ohly et al, 2010, p. 41). Networking harnesses the power of creativity within the social process.

Creativity is vital for global organizations, which must continually adapt to the shifting environment (Ohly, et al, 2010). The use of creativity provides a competitive response to changes in the marketplace. It is "openness to experience and practical problem solving" (Klonoski, 2012, p. 413). A study by Reese, Lee, Cohen, and Puckett revealed that creative ability did not diminish with age; however, it did undergo qualitative changes (Klonoski, 2012). The study concluded "that the middle aged group performed better than their younger counterparts in terms of ideational fluency, flexibility and originality. Self-perception of creativity does not diminish with age

[but] becomes more uniquely individualistic and complex" (Klonoski, 2012, p. 412). This presents a challenge for global organizations as Generation Y and Z enter the workforce, a workforce that was once dominated by the Baby Boomers. The Millennials, also known as Generation Y, or Gen Y, are "history's first 'always connected' generation. Steeped in digital technology and social media, they treat their multi-tasking hand-held gadgets with reverence" (Demirdjian, 2012, p. 1). While they may be more tech-savvy than their predecessors, they do not necessarily have the advantage when it comes to creativity. "Gen Z kids will grow up with a highly sophisticated media and computer environment and will be more Internet savvy and expert than their Gen Y forerunners" (Schroer, n.d.). Organizations must create an environment of collaborative networking where the young and technologically savvy can mix with the middle-aged and not-so-technologically savvy in order to maximize creativity and the generation of ideas. Incorporating social media into their strategic networking plan will provide organizations with an innovative method for harnessing the collective creativity of their personnel and yield competitive advantage. While organizational leaders

must carefully consider the implementation of creativity and innovation, they must do so with extreme awareness. Innovation and creativity present opportunities to share information and collaborate across a global spectrum. They also present the opportunity for ethical breaches.

Values and Ethics

Technology has placed a plethora of information in the palm of one's hand that must be guarded with PIN numbers and encryption software. Data can be snatched out of the air. Smartphones can easily be altered for nefarious purposes. "Making ethical decisions is a common task now in the realm of personal technology" (Mollman, 2008). Organizations have been plagued by the ethical failures of their leaders. Headlines abound with stories detailing the misplaced direction of leaders' moral compasses. "Organizations need values" (S. Kuczmarski, & T. Kuczmarski, 1995, p. 4). Leaders must instill a set of values and adhere to them. Furthermore, as organizations continue to rely on technology for the transmission and dissemination of information in conjunction with interorganizational networking, it is imperative that a clearly defined set of values is communicated and enforced. "Values are defined as the core set of beliefs and principles deemed to be desirable (by groups) of individuals while ethics are defined as the conception of what is right and fair conduct or behavior" (Joyner & Payne, 2002, p. 299). In other words, values help to form ethics, and ethics help us determine what is right or wrong as compared to a universally accepted standard. Of course, there is certainly room for variation and interpretation based on cultural standards and norms. Generally speaking, the expectation of an ethical standard exists in organizations.

"Ethics comprises complex ideas, applications, and interpretations about not only what is right and wrong, but also why things are considered right and wrong" (Bishop, 2013, p. 636). It is the 'why' that is of utmost concern for leaders because it infers a measure of variation, which indicates ethics is subject to interpretation. This interpretation could be based on changes in business practice, shifting value alignment, or social standardization. For example, marriage has undergone a restructuring in the last decade, and many young people today believe it is an unnecessary ritual. "A changing worldwide social outlook is adding to the demise of marital relationships, and declining religious values continue to break down the walls of wedlock" (Toews, 2014). The once-ethical standard that necessitated the social institution of marriage is rapidly declining. The collapse of the housing market in 2008 brought to light just how severe the industry's ethical erosion was. In addition to fraudulently manipulating financial documents in order to fund mortgages, more than a third of loan officers at Ameriquest habitually engaged in the use of illegal drugs in order stay awake and work longer hours to earn more money (McLean & Nocera, 2010).

Interestingly, the collective ethical failures mentioned above were the direct result of a shift in values, which can be grouped into three underlying dimensions:

> Internal values (self-fulfillment, self-respect, and sense of accomplishment); external values (security, sense of belonging, warm relationships with others, and being-well respected); and interpersonal values (fun and enjoyment in life and excitement). In general, internal values do not require the judgments or opinions of others. These values are predominantly internally motivated, and individuals who rate internal values highly believe that they can influence or control outcomes. In contrast, external values generally require the presence, judgments, or opinions of others.

> Interpersonal values combine some aspects of both internal and external values; however, by definition, they focus upon interactions between people. People who consider interpersonal values important might be more likely to place a higher value on dyadic relationships and, perhaps, might care more about the other person's opinion or evaluations (Kropp, Lavack, & Silvera, 2005, p. 11).

Interpersonal values are particularly applicable to networking since they have a direct bearing on ethical relationships, which form the foundation of networking. Mele (2009) observed, "Four elements can be distinguished in the practice of networking, which are highly relevant for an ethical perspective: (1) intention; (2) exchange of resources; (3) the exercise of power of each actor toward other actors; and (4) the behavioral and ideological influence within a network" (p. 493). Networking is a powerful resource. Ideas and information can be communicated at will. Lapses in ethics and shifting values can infect organizations and be unwittingly transmitted through networking channels. As such, organizational leaders must instill values in their people and must embody them in their actions. Organizations of the future will rely more heavily on networking and technology. Therefore, a strong ethical code is required.

The Future of Organizational Design

Globalization is ushering in the future, and organizations need to embrace new ways of conducting business. The speed of business has quickened and will continue to accelerate. Businesses will continue to become more demographically diverse as the workforce changes. "Companies will hire globally and workers will move internationally to follow opportunities. It also means that jobs can exist in one location while the worker is in another" (Watson, 2008, p. 258). More people will work from home in the future. Virtual meetings will be the norm rather than the exception. Videoconferences will be held via handheld mobile devices. The proliferation of technology will change the way organizations conduct business. At the same time, it will have the effect of isolating workers, who will rely on electronic media to communicate.

Leapfrogging from one job to another after a few years of employment in order to zigzag one's way up the ladder of success is a current pattern in the business environment. In the future, "workers will need to change jobs with increasing frequency to stay employed in 2040" (Cornish, 2004, p. 32). This will no doubt affect organizations' ability to maintain consistency and stability. Establishing a flexible framework will be paramount for survival and success. Sanchez (1997) argues that organizations of the future will be constructed via modular architecture. In regard to modular architecture, he contends, "The speed of organizational reconfiguration in response to a changing environment can be increased, thereby enhancing the organization's strategic flexibility" (Sanchez, 1997, p. 86). The pace of change will continue to increase, and organizations must be poised to respond and adapt quickly.

As organizations adapt their structure to changes in the environment and adjust to a mobile, isolated workforce, communication will cease to be linear. That is, it will become multidirectional and transcend established boundaries. The increased reliance on technology as the accepted medium of communication will all but eliminate existing organizational barriers and create an intricate, interconnected networking system. Seufert, Georg, and Bach (1999) observed, "Organizations are changing more and more from well-structured and manageable systems into interwoven network systems with blurred boundaries" (p. 180). Globalization is redefining the structure of organizations and changing standard operating procedures. Virtual organizations and relationships will become increasingly more common. Relationships now contain a major virtual element because people spend more of their social lives online (Brown, 2011). This will have a tremendous impact on commerce, particularly as the younger generation enters the workforce.

> Young people everywhere link up through IM, Twitter, blogs, smartphones, and social networking sites that are proliferating at an accelerating rate. This is a critical point for businesses to understand. The emerging generation is part of what is, in essence, a vast new cross-border empire. It is marked by an instant awareness of what's new, what's hot, what's desirable-and what's not (Brown, 2011, p. 30).

Connecting and communicating virtually will depend on technology as a mode of transmission. However, the underlying cause that will make it effective is networking—the development and cultivation of relationships.

Whether face-to-face or in the virtual world, connectivity between people will be based on relationships—the social interaction between people. Though in the future words may be typed and never actually spoken in person, they will still form relationships and networks. "Relationships developed through networking are based on an exchange among concerned parties" (Kim, 2013, p. 123). The timely exchange of information is vital to organizational success. Networks provide the catalyst for the free flow of information via both virtual and in-person communication. They serve as modular building blocks that can be easily interchanged by organizational leaders in order to maximize individual potential and ability in relationship to the whole. The use of networks as a means of information dissemination creates an internal and external dependency that affects all users (James & Yukl, 1993). This interdependency adds strength to the organization because it connects leaders to the entire construct, which is comprised of local and global employees, as well as external sources. Networking delivers instant communication that can retrieve the right information at the right time. It is the future of organizational infrastructures. And it will provide the mechanism to select the next leader.

Who's Next?

Periodically, corporate executives are swooned in an effort to secure their vast experience and 'save' the organization. Much like the trading that occurs at the end of football season, CEOs switch companies with regular frequency. In the process, they negotiate hefty salaries because the pool of qualified people is usually rather small, which gives them tremendous bargaining power. The future success of the organization is placed upon a single individual who is typically charismatic. Unfortunately "much less emphasis is placed on the company's strategic situation and how appropriate the background of the candidate is" (Khurana, 2002, p. 20). In other words, it is more acceptable to hire a 'brand name' than it is someone who actually understands the company. This is how many companies operate and conduct succession planning. After all, "quality attracts quality" (Khurana, 2002, p. 129).

No matter the company, a succession plan is a necessary and vital element of the strategic plan. Organizations change; people move on to other interests; some retire. Mission and vision change too, based on factors in the external environment. A succession plan is more than a contingency plan, which exists in the event something goes wrong, or something unexpected happens. Succession planning involves evaluating the future needs of the organization and planning accordingly by developing current employees (Sambrook, 2005). The leader today may not necessarily be the leader who is needed tomorrow. Rothwell (2005) noted, "As globalization exerts increasing influence, [the] one size fits all approaches will be increasingly out of step with good business practice" (p. 50). Manning the organizational helm for a prolonged duration is becoming increasingly rare. Technology is changing the way organizations conduct business and what business they conduct. Change means new ideas and new vision.

Succession planning begins the day a new leader takes the reigns, for at some point change will be necessary. The global landscape will dictate the requirements for a new leader. When it came to identifying a successor, Elkin, Smith, and Zhang (2012) noted, "Three first-order characteristics stood out: full understanding of the community...and networking skills and strong relationships. A lesser second-order set of characteristics was evident. They were problem solving and practical skills, good communication skills and verbal expressiveness" (p. 43). The ability to network and develop relationships is a critical ability for leaders, particularly those who ascend to the top of the organization. Successful leaders will serve their networks, which can be quite taxing. This is why it is incumbent upon leaders to incorporate rest into their daily lives.

Our fast-paced society accelerates exponentially as technology increases the proliferation of information. Organizational leaders are wont to keep up but are not immune from burnout. Our modern society practically mandates the preoccupation with career success at all costs. "Societies focused on career success tend to be more materialistic, emphasizing the acquisition of money and things. In contrast, societies focused more on quality of life emphasize relationships, concern for others, and overall quality of life" (Philips & Gully, 2011, p. 517). Servant networking is not conducive to the United States' society. However, by leading with purpose and conviction in the name of service to others, leaders can shift their focus to quality-of-life matters such as relationships and others.

Servant Networking: Opening the Box

Servant networking is based on the theory of servant leadership in which leaders develop the desire to serve others. It extends leadership and service by harnessing the power of networking to connect others without thought of personal gain. Specifically, it mandates service as a means of leadership, followership, and networking with the end goal of linking the right people together for their greater good. This theory is particularly relevant in the field of leadership because as globalization continues to envelop the world, connect countries, blur cultural boundaries, and change the way organizations operate, networks will become a critical component of success. Organizations of the future must open the box and unpack a self-contained flexible leadership model capable of adapting to an ever-changing environment. Servant networking meets this requirement.

First, servant networking is self-sustaining because the more individuals give, the more they receive. As such, it is perfectly suited to provide infrastructure within an organization by circumventing the many layers present in traditional structures. Second, technology has made instant and constant connectivity possible. Harnessing this power to connect others in the name of service will enhance strategic thinking and ultimately strategic planning. Third, servant networking combines an already existing system, networking, with leadership theory, servant leadership, in order to capitalize on human need. Its use can permeate the culture of an organization and create an environment where people genuinely care about others. Fourth, globalization has connected the world. The once face-to-face practice of networking and building relationships has taken on a digital dimension where serving others can provide tremendous advantage. Fifth, technology has created the first 'always connected' generation and thrown them in the mix with their seniors, who have begun to adapt to innovation. Cross-generational service via networking will bolster creativity and empower innovation. Sixth, the future belongs to technology. Interpersonal relationships will exist in the confines of social media, where meeting others' needs will remain necessary. Seventh, the leaders of future organizations will need to be more than just charismatic. They will need to be connected to the right people and serve their needs.

So, what's inside the box? Nothing! There is no formal structure because servant networking is based purely on willingly and freely serving others through relationships and connections. It is a personal commitment where humility replaces pride and sacrifice substitutes for self-interest. The box merely represents the concept that leadership cannot be compartmentalized and packaged into neat little components that when arranged properly function as a cohesive unit. The empty box symbolizes two things. One, servant networking is only bound by the constraints of those who practice it. The limitations reside in the individual's willingness to serve. Two, it is up to the individual to choose what to place in the box. That is, the service and connections are made at the discretion of the individual. Servant networking is mutually beneficial. Although reciprocity is the foundation of successful networking, servant networking is performed without this expectation. It is done purely out of concern for others, which makes it adaptable and viable for organizations as a structure, culture, and strategy. The only package necessary is the box—an empty vessel that symbolizes how much we have to offer others if we will only take the time to fill it!

References

Ali, A. J. (2001). Globalization: The great transformation. *Advances in Competitiveness Research, 9*(1), 1-9. Retrieved from http://0-search.proquest.com.library.regent.edu/docview/211369540?accountid=13479

Ardalan, K. (2009). Globalization and culture: Four paradigmatic views. *International Journal of Social Economics, 36*(5), 513-534. doi:http://dx.doi.org/10.1108/03068290910954013

Barbuto, J. E., Jr, & Wheeler, D. W. (2006). Scale development and construct clarification of servant leadership. *Group & Organization Management, 31*(3), 300-326. Retrieved from http://0-search.proquest.com.library.regent.edu/docview/203373307?accountid=13479

Belardo, S., Duchessi, P., & Coleman, J. R. (1994). A strategic decision support system at Orell Fussli. *Journal of Management Information Systems, 10*(4), 135-135. Retrieved from http://0-search.proquest.com.library.regent.edu/docview/218948905?accountid=13479

Bell, C. R. (2002). *Mangers as mentors: Building partnerships for learning.* San Francisco, CA: Berrett-Koehler Publishers, Inc.

Bennett, J., Owers, M., Pitt, M., & Tucker, M. (2010). Workplace impact of social networking. *Property Management, 28*(3), 138-148. doi:http://dx.doi.org/10.1108/02637471011051282

Bishop, W. H. (2013). *Going home: A networking survival guide.* USA: Xulon Press.

Bishop, W. H. (2014). The necessity of unification in globalization. *Leadership Advance Online, XXV,* 1-11.

Bishop, W. H. (2013). The role of ethics in 21st century organizations. *Journal of Business Ethics, 118*(3), 635-637. doi:http://dx.doi.org/10.1007/s10551-013-1618-1

Block, P. (1981). *Flawless consulting: A guide to getting your experience used.* San Francisco, CA: Pfieffer.

Bonn, I. (2005). Improving strategic thinking: A multilevel approach. *Leadership & Organization Development Journal, 26*(5), 336-354. Retrieved from http://0-

search.proquest.com.library.regent.edu/docview/226927160?accountid=13479

Boone, L. W., & Makhani, S. (2012). Five necessary attitudes of a servant leader. *Review of Business, 33*(1), 83-96. Retrieved from http://0-search.proquest.com.library.regent.edu/docview/1367068417?accountid=13479

Brown, A. (2011). Relationships, community, and identity in the new virtual society. *The Futurist, 45*(2), 29-31,34. Retrieved from http://0-search.proquest.com.library.regent.edu/docview/850509430?accountid=13479

Camplin, J. C,C.S.P., C.P.E.A. (2009). Volunteers leading volunteers. *Professional Safety, 54*(5), 36-42. Retrieved from http://0-search.proquest.com.library.regent.edu/docview/200342763?accountid=13479

Chaleff, I. (2009). *The courageous follower: Standing up to and for our leaders.* San Francisco, CA: Berrett-Koehler Publishers, Inc.

Charan, R. (1991). How networks reshape organizations - for results. *Harvard Business Review, 69*, 104. Retrieved from http://0-

search.proquest.com.library.regent.edu/docview/227839215?accountid=13479

Cialdini R. The uses (and abuses) of influence. *Harvard Business Review*. July 2013, 91(7/8):76-81.

Clayton, M. (2011). *Brilliant influence: What brilliant influencers know, do and.* New York, NY: Prentice Hall.

Cornish, E. (2004). *Futuring: The exploration of the future.* Bethsaida, MD: World Future Society.

Daft, R. L. (2007). *Organizational theory and design.* Mason, OH: Thomson.

De Kluyver, C. A. & Pearce II, J. A. (2009). *Strategy: A view from the top.* Upper Saddle River, NJ: Pearson.

Demirdjian, Z. S. (2012). The millennial generation's mindset: Susceptibility to economic crisis. *The Business Review, Cambridge, 19*(2), 2-I,II. Retrieved from http://0-search.proquest.com.library.regent.edu/docview/1021058856?accountid=13479

Elkin, G., Smith, K., & Zhang, H. (2012). Succession planning in the third sector in New Zealand. *New Zealand Journal of Employment Relations (Online),*

37(3), 34-49. Retrieved from http://0-search.proquest.com.library.regent.edu/docview/1413251527?accountid=13479

Fullam, C., Lando, A. R., Johansen, M. L., Reyes, A., & Szaloczy, D. M. (1998). The triad of empowerment: Leadership, environment, and professional traits. *Nursing Economics, 16*(5), 254-7, 253. Retrieved from http://0-search.proquest.com.library.regent.edu/docview/236930148?accountid=13479

Goldman, E. F. (2007). Strategic thinking at the top. *MIT Sloan Management Review, 48*(4), 75. Retrieved from http://0-search.proquest.com.library.regent.edu/docview/224968640?accountid=13479

Graen, G. B. & Uhl-Bien, M. (1991). *The transformation of professionals into self-managing and partially self-designing contributors: Toward a theory of leadership making.* Retrieved from: http://digitalcommons.unl.edu/cgi/viewcontent.cgi?article=1015&context=managementfacpub

Graetz, F. (2002). Strategic thinking versus strategic planning: Towards understanding the complementarities. *Management Decision, 40*(5), 456. Retrieved from http://0-search.proquest.com.library.regent.edu/docview/212061389?accountid=13479

Grenny, J., Maxfield, D., & Shimberg, A. (2008). How to have influence. *MIT Sloan Management Review, 50*(1), 47-52. Retrieved from http://0-search.proquest.com.library.regent.edu/docview/224973968?accountid=13479

Guadalupe, M., & Wulf, J. (2010). The flattening firm and product market competition: The effect of trade liberalization on corporate hierarchies. *American Economic Journal of Applied Economics, 2*(4), 105-127. doi: http://dx.doi.org/10.1257/app.2.4.105

Hamel, G. (2011). First, let's fire all the managers. *Harvard Business Review, 89*(12), 48-60.

Huang, X., Mehmet, M. K., & Roger, G. S. (2010). The impact of organizational structure on mass customization capability: A contingency view. *Production and Operations Management, 19*(5), 515-530. Retrieved from http://0-search.proquest.com.library.regent.edu/docview/755015056?accountid=13479

Hughes, R. L. & Beatty, K. C. (2005). *Becoming a strategic leader: Your role in your organization's enduring success.* San Francisco, CA: John Wiley & Sons.

James, M., & Yukl, G. (1993). Managerial level and subunit function as determinants of networking behavior in organizations. *Group & Organization Studies (1986-1998), 18*(3), 328. Retrieved from http://0-search.proquest.com.library.regent.edu/docview/232776086?accountid=13479

Jeffrey, A. O., & Brian, D. S. (2003). The limits of structural change. *MIT Sloan Management Review, 45*(1), 77-82. Retrieved from http://0-search.proquest.com.library.regent.edu/docview/224964784?accountid=13479

Johnson, R. L. (2011). Corporate strategy and the social networking phenomena. *Journal of Service Science (Online), 4*(2), 1. Retrieved from http://0-search.proquest.com.library.regent.edu/docview/1418717015?accountid=13479

Joyner, B. E., & Payne, D. (2002). Evolution and implementation: A study of values, business ethics and corporate social responsibility. Journal of Business Ethics, 41 (4), 297-311. Retrieved from: http://0-search.proquest.com.library.regent.edu/docview/197994208?Accountid=13479.

Kelley, R. (1992). *The power of followership.* New York, NY: Doubleday.

Khurana, R. (2002). *Searching for a corporate savior.* Princeton, NJ: Princeton University Press.

Kim, S. (2013). Networking enablers, constraints and dynamics: A qualitative analysis. *Career Development International, 18*(2), 120-138. doi:http://dx.doi.org/10.1108/CDI-04-2012-0051

Klonoski, R., J.D. (2012). How important is creativity? the impact of age, occupation and cultural background on the assessment of ideas. *Journal of Applied Business Research, 28*(3), 411-425. Retrieved from http://0-search.proquest.com.library.regent.edu/docview/1020618116?accountid=13479

Kropp, F., Lavack, A. M., & Silvera, D. H. (2005). Values and collective self-esteem as predictors of consumer susceptibility to interpersonal influence among university students. *International Marketing Review, 22*(1), 7-33. Retrieved from http://0-search.proquest.com.library.regent.edu/docview/224303227?accountid=13479

Kuczmarski, S. S. & Kuczmarski, T. D. (1995). *Values-based leadership: Rebuilding employee commitment, performance, and productivity.* Englewood Cliffs, NJ: Prentice Hall.

Leavitt, H. J. (2004). *Top down: Why hierarchies are here to stay and how to manage them more effectively.* Retrieved from: Google Books.

Lewis, T., & Wright, G. A. (2012). How does creativity complement today's currency of innovation? *Journal of Strategic Innovation and Sustainability, 7*(3), 9-15. Retrieved from http://0-search.proquest.com.library.regent.edu/docview/1021381505?accountid=13479

Liedtka, J. M. (1998). Linking strategic thinking with strategic planning. *Strategy & Leadership, 26*(4), 30-35. Retrieved from http://0-search.proquest.com.library.regent.edu/docview/194364332?accountid=13479

Linehan, M., & Scullion, H. (2008). The development of female global managers: The role of mentoring and networking. *Journal of Business Ethics, 83*(1), 29-40. doi:http://dx.doi.org/10.1007/s10551-007-9657-0

Marquardt, M. J. & Berger, N. O. (). *Global leaders for the 21st century.* Albany, NY: State University of New York Press.

McCall, Jr., M. W., & Hollenbeck, G. P. (2002). *Developing global executives: The lessons of international experience.* Cambridge, MA: Harvard Business School Press.

McLean, T. & Nocera, J. (2010). *All the devils are here: The hidden history of the financial crisis.* New York, NY: Penguin Group.

Melé, D. (2009). The practice of networking: An ethical approach. *Journal of Business Ethics, 90*, 487-503. doi:http://dx.doi.org/10.1007/s10551-010-0602-2

Miller, C. (1995). *The empowered leader: 10 keys to servant leadership.* Nashville, TN: B&H Publishing Group.

Mintzberg, H., Ahlstrand, B., & Lampel, J. (1998). *Strategy safari.* New York, NY: Free Press.

Mollman, S. (2008). *Technology posing ethical questions.* Retrieved from: http://www.cnn.com/2008/BUSINESS/09/25/digital.ethics/

Northouse, P. G. (2007). *Leadership theory and practice.* Thousand Oaks, CA: Sage Publications.

Ohly, S., Kase, R., & Skerlavaj, M. (2010). Networks for generating and for validating ideas: The social side of creativity. *Innovation: Management, Policy & Practice, 12*(1), 41-52. Retrieved from http://0-search.proquest.com.library.regent.edu/docview/507819728?accountid=13479

Philips, J. & Gully, S. (2011). *Organizational behavior: Tools for success.* Retrieved from Google Books.

Rosen, R. (2000). *Global literacies.* New York, NY: Simon & Schuster.

Rothewell, W. J. (2005). *Effective succession planning: Ensuring leadership continuity and building talent from within.* New York, NY: American Management Association.

Sambrook, S. (2005). Exploring succession planning in small, growing firms. *Journal of Small Business and Enterprise Development, 12*(4), 579-594.

Retrieved from http://0-search.proquest.com.library.regent.edu/docview/219242974?accountid=13479

Sanchez, R. (1997). Preparing for an uncertain future: Managing organizations for strategic flexibility. *International Studies of Management & Organization, 27*(2), 71-94. Retrieved from http://0-search.proquest.com.library.regent.edu/docview/224077271?accountid=13479

Sawant, N., Li, J., & Wang, J. Z. (2011). Automatic image semantic interpretation using social action and tagging data. *Multimedia Tools and Applications, 51*(1), 213-246. doi:http://dx.doi.org/10.1007/s11042-010-0650-8

Schroer, W. J. (n.d.). *Generations X, Y, Z and the others.* Retrieved from: http://www.socialmarketing.org/newsletter/features/generation3.htm

Setyawati, I. M., Mohd Noor, M. S., & Mohammad, B. S. (2011). Effects of learning, networking and innovation adoption on successful entrepreneurs in central java, indonesia. *International Journal of Business and Social Science, 2*(5) Retrieved from http://0-search.proquest.com.library.regent.edu/docview/904528145?accountid=13479

Seufert, A., Georg, v. K., & Bach, A. (1999). Towards knowledge networking. *Journal of Knowledge Management, 3*(3), 180-190. Retrieved from http://0-search.proquest.com.library.regent.edu/docview/230337069?accountid=13479

Silverman, E. (2012). *Who's the boss? There isn't one.* Retrieved from: http://online.wsj.com/article/SB10001424052702303379204577474953586383604.html

Sinclaire, J. K., & Vogus, C. E. (2011). Adoption of social networking sites: An exploratory adaptive structuration perspective for global organizations. *Information Technology and Management, 12*(4), 293-314. doi:http://dx.doi.org/10.1007/s10799-011-0086-5

Spears, L. (1996). Reflections on Robert K. Greenleaf and servant-leadership. *Leadership & Organization Development Journal, 17*(7), 33-35. Retrieved from http://0-

search.proquest.com.library.regent.edu/docview/226920195?accountid=13479

Toews, J. (2014). *Is marriage outdated?* Retrieved from: http://realtruth.org/articles/110222-002-marriage.html

Watson, R. (2008). *Future files: The 5 trends that will shape the next 50 years.* Boston, MA: Nicholas Brealey Publishing.

Wills, G. (1994). Networking and its leadership processes. *Leadership & Organization Development Journal, 15*(7), 19. Retrieved from http://0-search.proquest.com.library.regent.edu/docview/226919569?accountid=13479

Zeffane, R. (1994). Inter-organizational alliance and networking: Dynamics, processes and technology? *Leadership & Organization Development Journal, 15*(7), 28. Retrieved from http://0-search.proquest.com.library.regent.edu/docview/226917745?accountid=13479

Zeffane, R. (1995). The widening scope of inter-organizational networking: Economic, sectoral and social dimensions. *Leadership & Organization Development Journal, 16*(4), 26. Retrieved from http://0-search.proquest.com.library.regent.edu/docview/226919744?accountid=13479

Zidbits Media (n.d.). *Why do ducks fly in a V?* Retrieved from: http://zidbits.com/2010/12/why-do-ducks-fly-in-a-v/

Printed in Great Britain
by Amazon